Dedicated to the Glory of God
and for the Children of God
so that they may have eyes to see!

Acknowledgements:
To my most precious gifts: Greg, Chris, and Alex - thank you God for entrusting them to my care, and to my loving wife, DeSha, for her belief in me, and most importantly for her trust in God. To my family, guides, and mentors: Mary, Carmen, Joann, Kent, Rob, Tom, Pat, Jeff & PJ; and to the artist Travis Hanson, who has helped this dream become reality. To the many angels God has sent my way to make this book happen: Jim and Sheila, Carl and Ellie, Carolyn, Naomi, Susan, Sonya, Tina, Mattie, Elizabeth, and to the countless authors and teachers, too many to name, for sharing their wisdom and teaching me how to see.

For further information please contact Carmen J. Viola at the website: heartofdiscipleship.com

ISBN 978-1-4507-9720-7

Printed in China
First Edition September 2015

the Heart of Discipleship

by Carmen J. Viola
illustrated by Travis Hanson

Blessing's

How To Use This Book

What does it mean to follow Jesus?
Explore Bible stories and concepts that become relavant for us today.

A MATTER OF PERSPECTIVE

Colors & Symbols

Explore how colors & symbols are used throughout the book

Your Perspective

What is being communicated to you personally?

Bible Readings

Read the corresponding scripture passages in your own Bible

Children's Corner

Questions that families & Sunday Schools can use to enhance a child's view of God's Story

Ancient Ideas

Ancient Context might shed some new light on the story

Points to Ponder

Questions that you and your group can use to further explore the Bible story and how it is relevant for you today

Concepts

Key words represent themes and ideas that run through these stories

In The Beginning...

I Am the Light of the World (John 8:12)

T.HANSON©2014

NOWHERE (*The Creation Story*)

Genesis 1:1-2:3; John 1:1-5

Points to Ponder:

God's intelligence is contained within all matter and energy (a thought from God becomes embodied spirit, a physical creation). We are all resurrected star-matter; as a star must die for carbon to be created. The universe in which we live is life in communion with God. Why is God compared to light? As we are created in God's image, do you believe we too are both matter and energy?

Do you believe the Universe is random? Do you believe everything is connected? Is God a He, She, It, or a We? We are both one and many. What does that mean?

During Creation, God created a day of rest. Why is it important to take a break each week from our daily routines? How does resting and focused breathing reset our bodies?

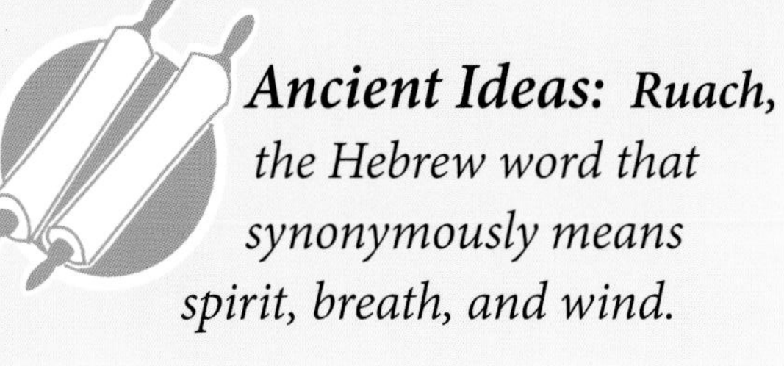

Ancient Ideas: *Ruach, the Hebrew word that synonymously means spirit, breath, and wind.*

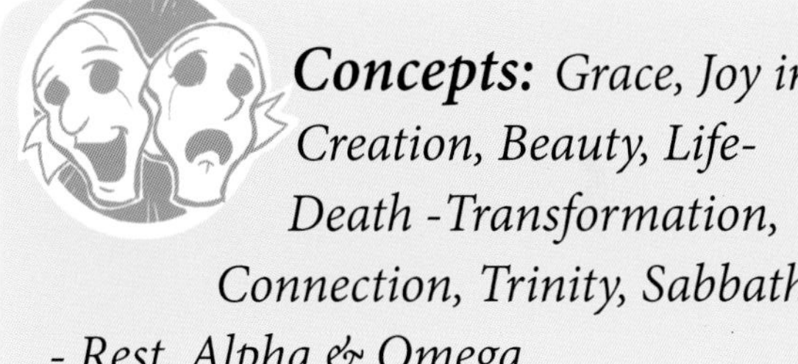

Concepts: *Grace, Joy in Creation, Beauty, Life-Death -Transformation, Connection, Trinity, Sabbath - Rest, Alpha & Omega*

Children's Corner:

Have you ever looked up at the stars?

Where do they all come from?

Why is breathing so important?

Why is it important to take a break from time to time?

VERY GOOD (Adam & Eve in the Garden)

Genesis 2:4-25; Genesis 3:1-23

Points to Ponder:

We are born male and female - God created them both in God's image. What does it mean to be an image bearer? Why was creation "very good" after we were created? What went wrong? What does it mean to have authority, but to also be vulnerable (naked)?

What does the serpent represent? What do the trees in the garden represent? What do Adam and Eve represent?

Does our ego separate us from God and from one another in some way?

Children's Corner:

How are boys and girls the same? How are they different? Is one better than the other?

What does it mean to obey your parents? Why is that important?

Did you ever get into trouble because you let someone or something influence you to do something bad, even though you knew better?

Do you know what responsibility and accountability mean?

Ancient Ideas: *"Adam" in Hebrew means humanity and alludes to the ground, earth (dirt); "Eve" means living.*

Concepts: *Beauty, Peace, Connection, Stewardship, Responsibility, Accountability, Co-Creation, Obedience, Shame, Blame, Sin, Evil*

T.HANSON
2014

PROMISE *(Noah)*
Genesis 9:7-17, Hebrews 10:16-25

Points to Ponder:

What does it mean to be in a relationship with all of creation?

What does it mean to trust God in the face of devastation?

As the Ark comes through the waters, the earth itself is renewed and life is re-created. Where else in the Bible does water symbolize death and resurrection?

Children's Corner:

Did you know that a rainbow and all its different colors come together to create white light? Light is one color and many colors at the same time. Can other things seem different but be alike in some ways? Like what?

What does it mean to make a promise? Do you keep your promises? Do you expect another person's promises to be kept?

How do you know if a relationship is good or bad?

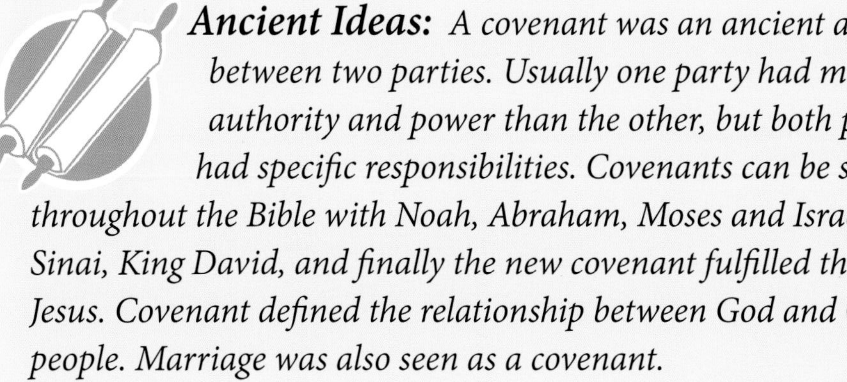

Ancient Ideas: *A covenant was an ancient agreement between two parties. Usually one party had more authority and power than the other, but both parties had specific responsibilities. Covenants can be seen throughout the Bible with Noah, Abraham, Moses and Israel at Sinai, King David, and finally the new covenant fulfilled through Jesus. Covenant defined the relationship between God and God's people. Marriage was also seen as a covenant.*

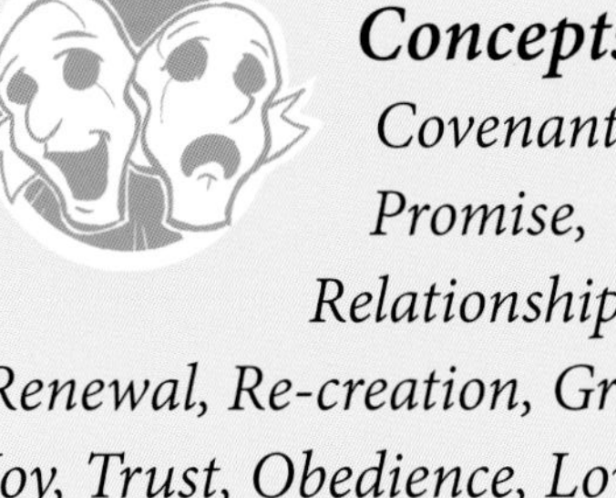

Concepts: *Covenant, Promise, Relationship, Renewal, Re-creation, Grace, Joy, Trust, Obedience, Love*

FATHER *(Abraham)*
Genesis 21:9-13; Romans 10:11-13

Points to Ponder:

People's names in the Bible often informed the audience of the story's intent and gave insight into a person's spirit. Reflect upon your own name; what does it mean and why was it chosen?

All three monotheistic religions (Christianity, Judaism, Islam) stem from Abraham. Who then are God's people? What does it mean to be a child in your own family? And what does it mean to be a child of God?

Ancient Ideas: *In Hebrew, "Abraham" means father of many; "Sarah" means princess; "Isaac" means he laughs; "Hagar" means stranger; and "Ishmael" means God hears.*

Concepts: *Covenant, Joy, Sorrow, Compassion, Jealousy, Trust, Obedience, Faith, Hope, Connections*

Children's Corner:

Are people the same or are they different? What about those in other countries? How are they different from us and how are they the same?

What do people everywhere have in common? Do we all come from the same ancestors?

How should we treat our brothers and sisters?

Have you ever felt jealous of your brothers and sisters?

ALIVE (Joseph)
Genesis 37:1-28; Matthew 26:14-16

Points to Ponder:

How much pressure is there to conform in the world? What does it mean to sell out? When is it good to conform and when can it be bad?

Do you envy someone else, their status, or their possessions? Do you live vicariously through someone else?

Have you followed your dreams (why or why not)? We all have a special song inside us, don't leave here with that song unsung. What is your special song? What are you passionate about? When do you feel most alive?

Children's Corner:

Who do you want to be like when you grow up? Why? Do you wish you were like someone else or that you had things that others have?

When is it good to follow others? When can it be a bad thing to follow others?

What does the word "passion" mean? Do you have a dream for yourself? What is it?

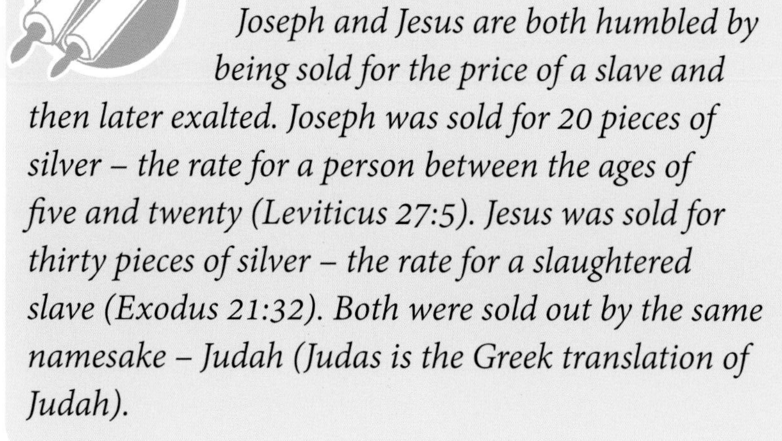

Ancient Ideas: *The price of a human slave was recorded in Mosaic Law. Joseph and Jesus are both humbled by being sold for the price of a slave and then later exalted. Joseph was sold for 20 pieces of silver – the rate for a person between the ages of five and twenty (Leviticus 27:5). Jesus was sold for thirty pieces of silver – the rate for a slaughtered slave (Exodus 21:32). Both were sold out by the same namesake – Judah (Judas is the Greek translation of Judah).*

Concepts: *Conforming, Selling Out, Envy, Jealousy, Dreams, Passion*

RICH & FAMOUS *(Moses & Pharaoh)*
Exodus 12:31-42

Points to Ponder:

What does it mean to be free? What does it mean to be a slave?

What gods and idols rule our lives and our society today?

When you feel powerless or are suffering, do you believe God hears your cry?

Do you hear the cry of others who are suffering in the world??

Ancient Ideas:
Ze'akah, *in Hebrew, means to cry out from the depths of one's being. God always hears the cry of God's children and those who are oppressed and suffering.*

Concepts: *Power, Doubt, The Kingdom of God, The Kingdom of Man, Slavery, Freedom, Power, Idols, Repent, Suffering, Prayer, Compassion*

Children's Corner:

Do you ever feel like you only do what other people want you to do? How does it feel to be bossed around?

When you get hurt, do your parents hear you when you cry? How do they treat you when you are hurt? How do you feel when someone else is crying?

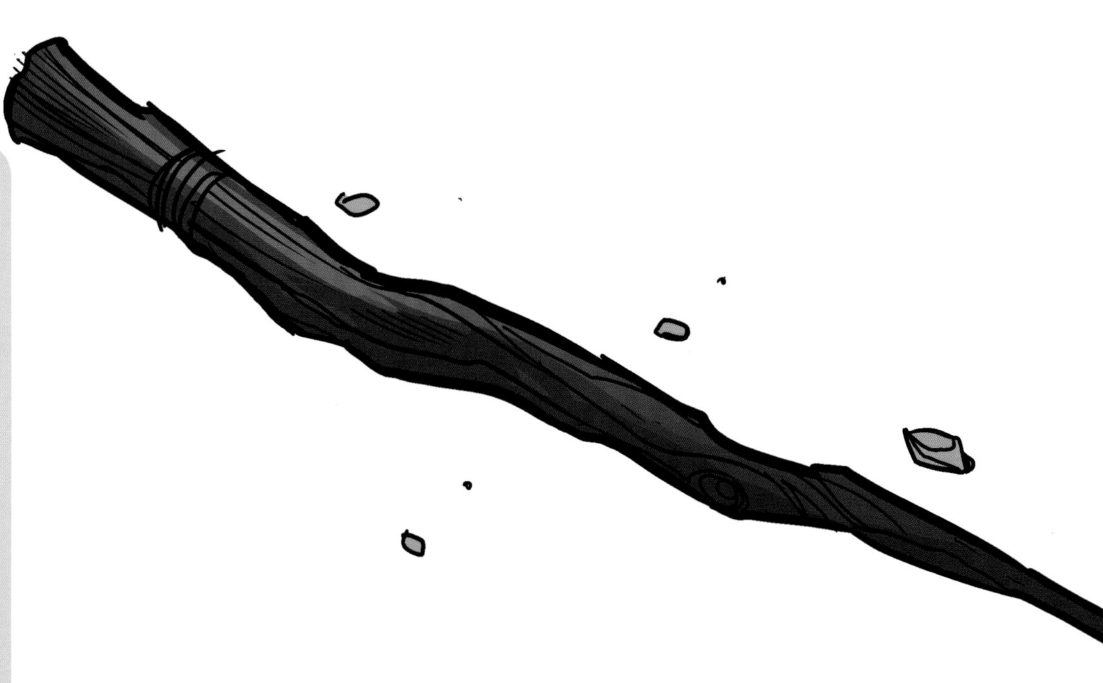

ARE WE THERE YET (*Deserts*)
Numbers 32:13; Deuteronomy 29:2-6; Nehemiah 9:19-21; John 14:27

Points to Ponder:

Why were God's people taken through the desert to freedom?

When God led His people into the desert, how did He use the experience to remove Egypt from His people? What does the desert represent?

Are there different seasons to the spiritual life?

What are the negatives and positives of a desert experience? Why do we feel uncomfortable being in a desert? Sharing your desert experiences with others lets you see the value and purpose of the experience.

Ancient Ideas: *The Desert in the ancient world was a paradox. It was a place of peril and danger, but also a place of refuge, solace, and provision. It is a place where God's people learned to trust God completely, a place where we are cleansed of our worldly influences and expectations.*

Concepts: *Absence, Temptation, Obedience, Lost, Alone, Idolatry, Doubt, Fear, Grief, Discipline, Testing, Peace, Trust, Solitude, Prayer, Patience, Acceptance, Openness*

Children's Corner:

Have you ever taken a long time to get somewhere?

Do you ever feel like you can't wait for something to happen?

What do you do in those "in-between" times while you are waiting?

LAND OF MILK AND HONEY *(The Judean Hillside)*
Isaiah 58:12; Acts 4:32-35; Genesis 1:26-27

Points to Ponder:

Can we truly be independent? How are we connected to God and everyone else? What are some examples?

Are we a community of MEs (self-reliant and alone) or WEs (Interdependent and Connected)? Do you believe God is a "we" or a "me?" What does it mean to live in a community? Do you believe that we are the sum of our relationships?

How do we find the land of milk and honey (the Kingdom of God) today?

Children's Corner:

How are you connected to your family, your neighbors and your school?

Is it fun for you to do something big all by yourself or is it easier to do something as a family if everyone is helping? What chores do you do that make it easier for your family to work together? What does your family share with one another? How can we share more with our neighbors?

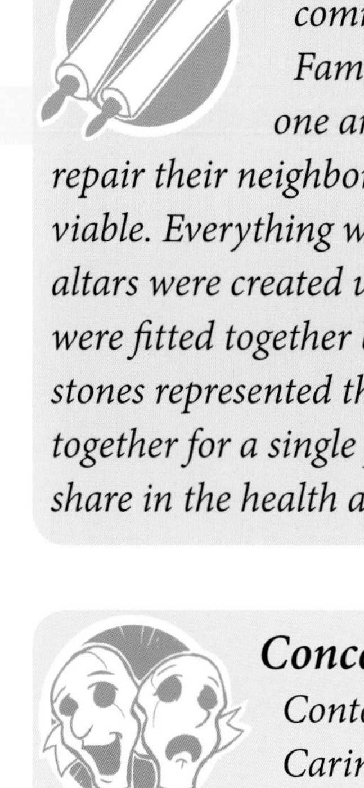

Ancient Ideas: *A* ***gan*** *was an ancient terraced community that was physically interdependent. Families would plant their crops vertically upon one another. The family below was required to repair their neighbor's wall above to keep the entire community viable. Everything was shared in kind. In ancient times, walls and altars were created using different sized unworked stones that were fitted together by hand to create the structure. The different stones represented the different people in the community all coming together for a single purpose, whether it was to worship God or share in the health and welfare of the community.*

Concepts: *Abundance, Interdependent, Just Enough, Contentment, Appreciation, Blessings, Sharing, Caring, Community, Responsibility, Accountability, Purpose, Harmony, Compassion*

GIVE ME STRENGTH *(Samson, The Greatest Commandment)*
Judges 16:15-31; Deuteronomy 6:3-12; Matthew 22:34-40; Mark 12:28-34

Points to Ponder:

How much do we rely on ourselves, others, or God on a day-to-day basis? Where does your strength come from?

What is the danger in being too successful and/or powerful? Can we forget God when times are good? What is the danger in that? Why is it so important to put God first in your life?

Children's Corner:

Can we do everything by ourselves? Can we fix all our own problems?

Try this: God is the creator (the number 1) and everything else is created (the number 0). If we put the number 1 first, everything after it has value, but if you put the zeroes first, the value of our lives is not increased. Talk about why it's so important to put God first in our lives and in our hearts.

Ancient Ideas: *The* ***Shema*** *(Deuteronomy 6) is the prayer that is uttered by all God's people upon waking and going to bed to remind us to place God in the center of our lives. In Hebrew,* ***Levav*** *(the heart) translates as intentions and desires,* ***Nephesh*** *(the soul) is who you are at your core, and* ***Mehodaha*** *(your mind) translates as all your possessions. So the* ***Shema*** *commands you to love God with your deepest desires, the sum of your story, and all of your stuff! In a sense, we need to bring everything we are to our relationship with God.*

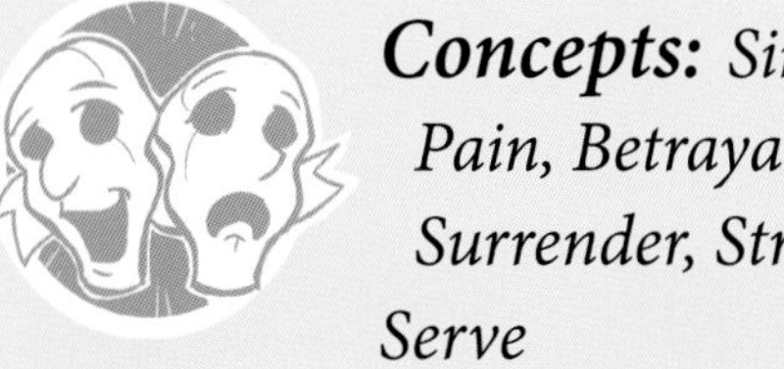

Concepts: *Sin, Ego, Power, Self-Reliance, Pain, Betrayal, Suffering, Broken, Surrender, Strength & Weakness, God First, Serve*

WE'VE GOT THIS (*David & Goliath*)

1 Samuel 17:1-50

Points to Ponder:

How much fear is generated in our society? What do you fear most? What is the face of that fear? Can we exaggerate fear?

How stressful is your life? Where does the stress come from? What does it mean to trust God in the face of overwhelming odds?

Can one person really make a difference? Can one person make a difference when God is with them? Can one person make a difference when others are supporting them?

Ancient Ideas: *The valley of Elah is a flat valley, located on the low hills of Judah. This valley was an important strategic coastal corridor controlling access to the cities of Bethlehem, Hebron, and Jerusalem.*

The Philistines, a battle-hardened people with superior weapons and armor, constantly threatened the Hebrews controlling this region. They represented power and might in the ancient world.

Concepts: *Fear, Power, Expectations, Trust, Appreciation*

Children's Corner:

Have you ever felt too small?

Have you ever felt bullied?

How does having someone to rely on or talk to help you overcome big challenges?

How can trusting in God help you when things seem too hard?

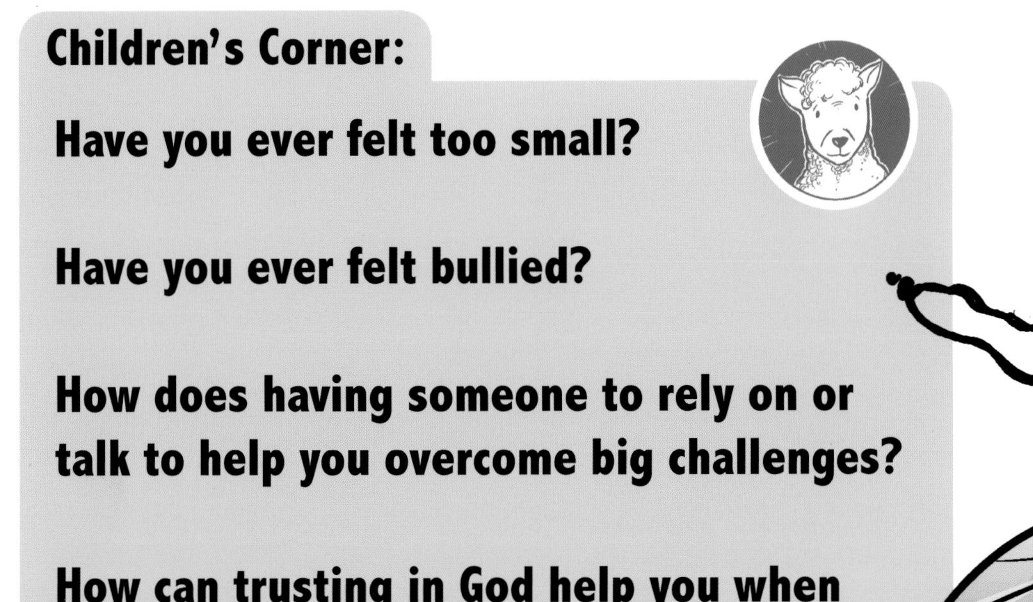

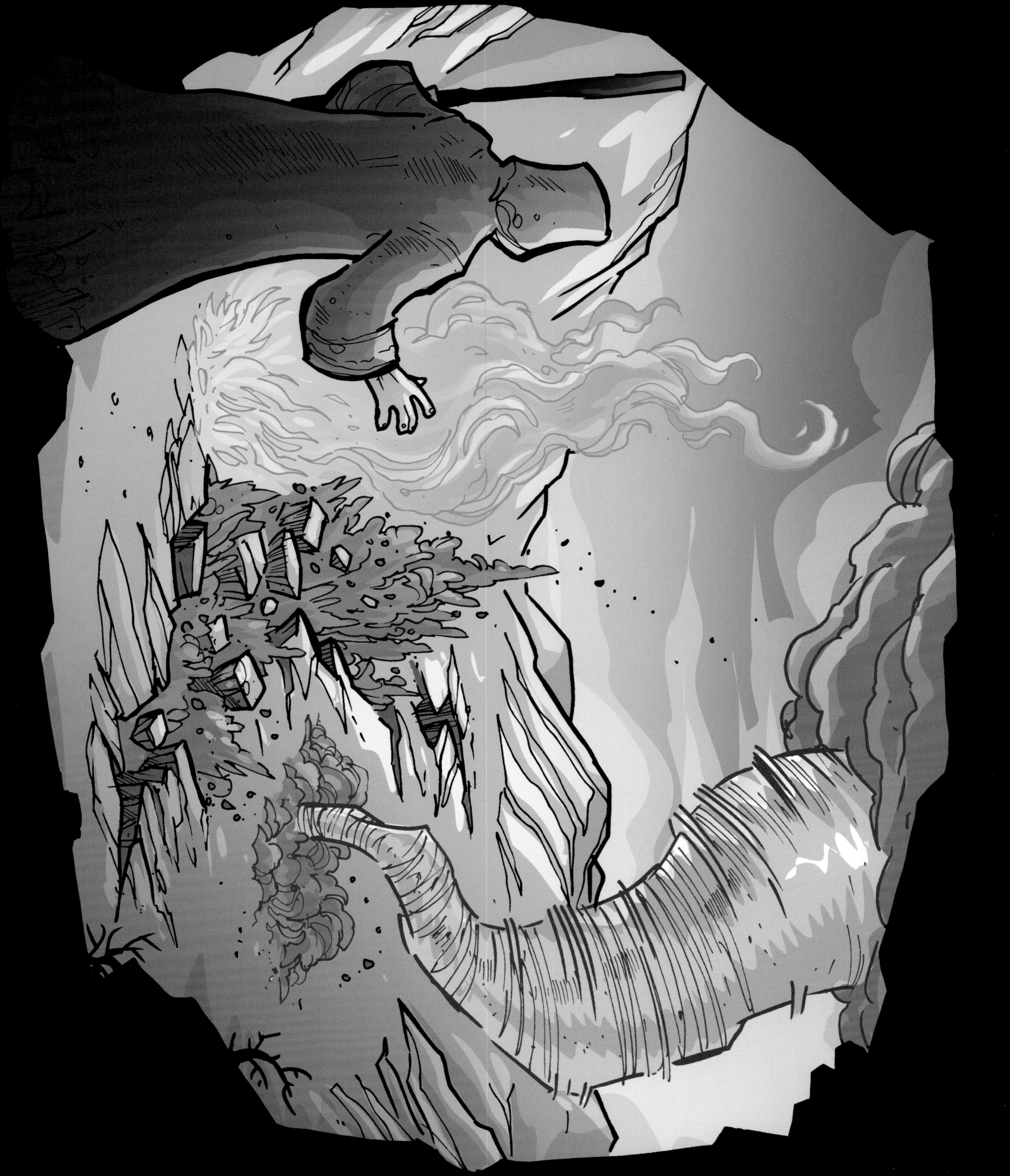

WHERE ARE YOU – WHERE AM I (Elijah)

1 Kings 19:11-13; Psalm 46; Luke 5:15-16

Points to Ponder:

How much noise and distraction is in your life? Can you hear God through the noise of today? What are some distractions in our lives? How do you meditate and pray? Are we talking at God or listening for God?

What keeps you from a deeper relationship with God? Where is God in your life? Where are you in God's life? Do we create space for God?

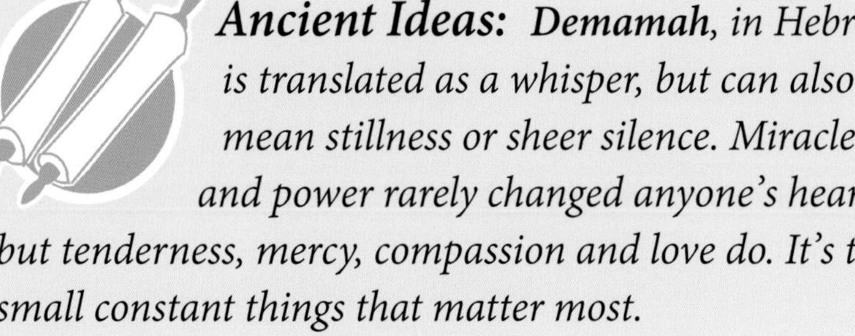

Ancient Ideas: ***Demamah****, in Hebrew, is translated as a whisper, but can also mean stillness or sheer silence. Miracles and power rarely changed anyone's heart; but tenderness, mercy, compassion and love do. It's the small constant things that matter most.*

Concepts: *Noise, Distraction, Fear, God's Presence, Silence, Listen, Prayer, Solitude*

Children's Corner:

Is there a lot of noise in your house? From what? Have you ever been really quiet?

Can we hear better when it's quiet? Are you always doing something? Is it nice to be still and quiet at times?

Why is prayer important?

T.HANSON 2014

REALLY (Jonah)

Jonah 4:1-10; Matthew 5:38-48; Luke 6:27-38

Points to Ponder:

Is life fair? Does God take sides?

What does it mean to love your enemy? Could you really do it?

What are your own prejudices and labels for others that keep you from loving all God's children?

Ancient Ideas: *The word "repent" in Greek is* ***metanoia****, which means to turn around or to change one's mind; to see things in a new or different way.*

Concepts: *Running Away, Hatred, Anger, Judging, Us vs. Them, Obedience, Fairness, Mercy, Forgiveness, Understanding*

Children's Corner:

What does being fair mean? Is life fair? How do you feel if you don't want to do something or go somewhere? How do you act?

Are there some people you just don't like? Can you love someone and not like them? Are there times when you don't like someone in your family? Do you still love them?

WHY *(Job)*

Job 42:1-6; Isaiah 41:10

Points to Ponder:

Do you believe God is a loving God? Is God an "if…then…" God, offering rewards and punishments according to your actions? Can you earn God's favor?

Why is there pain and suffering in the world? What does it mean to transcend the dual nature (opposites) of the world?

What is your own view of God? Can you imagine God in a bigger way? What does it mean to be in right relationship with God?

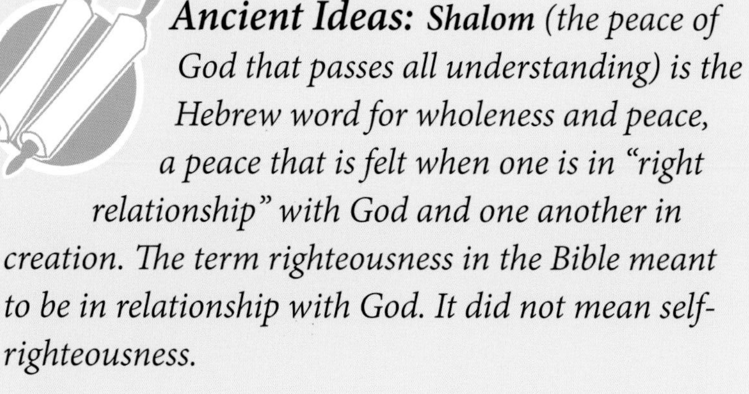

Ancient Ideas: ***Shalom*** *(the peace of God that passes all understanding) is the Hebrew word for wholeness and peace, a peace that is felt when one is in "right relationship" with God and one another in creation. The term righteousness in the Bible meant to be in relationship with God. It did not mean self-righteousness.*

Concepts: *Pain, Suffering, Forsaken, Alone, Doubt, Faith, Trust, God with Us, Presence, Humility, Redemption, Acceptance, Prayer*

Children's Corner:

Do you believe God loves you? What does it mean to have a relationship with God?

Do bad things happen sometimes? Like what? Why do you think bad things happen? Can you do anything about them? What can you do when something bad happens?

DO NOT BE AFRAID (*Annunciation*)
Luke 1:26-38; Matthew 1:18-25

Points to Ponder:

Why do God and God's messengers throughout the Bible say "Do Not Be Afraid?" How are fear and love opposites? Love is being open to God's will for you and the world. Fear is being closed to the possibility of trusting God.

Does being open to God lead to an easy path? How does receiving and sharing God bring new life to the barren places of the world? What are the risks involved in following God's will? Are you following God's will for you?

Ancient Ideas: *In ancient times couples were betrothed for a year while the husband made ready their dwelling - usually attached to his family's. Once finished, the young woman would leave her family and become part of the husband's family. Mary's acceptance of God's gift would have led her to be an outcast in her own community. Joseph in this culture should have shunned his betrothed.*

Concepts: *Fear, Awe, Trust, Acceptance. Obedience, Betrayal, Sacrifice, Protection, Provision, Open, Humble, Innocence, Love, New Life, Communion with God, Prayer*

Children's Corner:

Are you afraid of some things?
Can you be brave?

Do your parents ask you to do things that you are afraid of sometimes? Does doing them help you to grow?

When is fear good and when is fear bad?

JOY IN THE WORLD (*Birth of Jesus*)

Luke 2:1-20; Luke 3:23-38; Matthew 1:1-17

Points to Ponder:

Jesus' birth, as we picture it, is only found in Luke's gospel. Both Matthew and Luke begin their gospels by mentioning the genealogies of Jesus, yet they are different. Why do you think that is? What was Jesus' purpose in coming to us?

Where is the Kingdom of God? How is the Kingdom of God revealed?

Jesus was first presented to the shepherds who were the marginalized at that time. Why so? What do you think that means for us today?

What is Grace?

Ancient Ideas: *"Immanuel" means God with us. "Messiah" means the one anointed with oil and represented a King from the line of David from the tribe of Judah. Middle Eastern tribal culture holds hospitality to be an important part of their culture even today. Shepherds were considered to be lower class citizens. God consistently works through those at the margins of society. Abraham, Isaac, Jacob, Moses, and David were all shepherds.*

Concepts: *Unconditional Love, Joy, Hope, Peace, Awe & Wonder, Grace, Hospitality, Family, Connection*

Children's Corner:

Have you ever seen a newborn baby? What do they look like?

Do you like Christmas? What do you like about it? What is Christmas about? Why do you think Jesus came to us?

Have you heard of the word grace? What do you think it means?

WATER & FIRE (*Jesus' Baptism*)

Mark 1:1-14; Luke 3:21-22

Points to Ponder:

What does it mean to be baptized? Why is Baptism important?

What does it mean to repent?

What does it mean for your "self" to die?

Is purity more a result of a ritual or of changing your heart?

What is the community of God?

Ancient Ideas: *A* **mikveh** *was an ancient Hebrew ritual bath. Through immersion into this "living" water one could regain their ritual purity. John the Baptist was calling the Hebrews to repent and remember themselves as God's people. Through baptism, he was symbolically recounting the Exodus story by inviting people down into the water and up into new life as a child of God.*

Concepts: *Death & Transformation, Ego and Self, Baptism, New Life, Purity*

Children's Corner:

Were you baptized?

What do you think that means?

Do you belong to any groups?

What does it mean to belong?

COME FOLLOW ME (Jesus calls His Disciples)
Luke 5:1-11; Matthew 4:18-22; Mark 1:16-20; John 1:35-42

Points to Ponder:

What do you think these young men were thinking when they decided to drop everything and follow Jesus? What does it mean to follow Jesus?

How can we invite others to become fishers of people? Why should we invite others?

How do we foster the heart of a disciple? Why did Jesus pick ordinary people from ordinary places?

***Ancient Ideas:* Rabbi** *means teacher. In ancient Israel, the rabbi was the "rockstar" of his day and would interpret God's words for all the people. Different rabbis interpreted things differently. Rabbis would only take the best and brightest as their disciples. Disciples would be humble students who would follow the rabbi with the intent to become like the rabbi in time. The Rabbi Jesus, however, selected the "any bodies" from simple ordinary places.*

Concepts: *Follow, Obedience, Invite, Trust, Disciple, Worthy*

Children's Corner:

Why is it hard to listen sometimes? Why is it hard to follow the examples of others? To learn from your experience is smart; to learn from another's experiences is wise. What does that mean?

What does it mean to follow Jesus?

UNCONDITIONAL (The Woman at the Well)
John 4:4-42; John 13:34; Romans 8:34-39

Points to Ponder:

Have you ever felt not smart enough, not attractive enough, not good enough? What story do you believe about yourself? Where did your story come from? What if you lived as if you were not defined by your failures? What if you lived as though you were worthy of love?

How do you sabotage your own life? What conditional lenses do you see the world through? How can that limit your view of God? How can your view of God limit how you extend love to others, including yourself?

Ancient Ideas: *The woman in this story was the ultimate outsider. She was a nameless Samaritan woman, despised by the Hebrews and of no worth to a Hebrew male teacher. She was even marginalized by her own people due to her lifestyle. Despite this, Jesus met her where she was to offer her a glimpse of God's love. She was not valued in her culture but she was valued by Jesus.*

Concepts: *Grace, Worthy, Non-Judgmental, Acceptance, Hope, Freedom, Unconditional Love*

Children's Corner:

What does the word "unconditional" mean? What does it mean to love someone "with no strings attached?"

Do you find it easier to love people who look and act like you? Why is it important to love people who look and act differently than you? How do you think God loves us?

GARDENING (Parables of the Seeds)
Matthew 13:1-32; Mark 4:1-20; Luke 8:4-15

Points to Ponder:

Why did Jesus and His disciples scatter the good news of the Kingdom of God everywhere, and not just in fertile ground? What is the potential of a seed? What is the potential of a person?

The growth of a seed is a slow process; so too is the changing of our hearts. Have you let God into your heart? Changing your heart and the hearts of others is a process that begins with an open heart. Is your heart open to God, His word, and His love? How can we sow God's seeds in the world?

Ancient Ideas: *Mustard seed, a very quickly germinating seed, was the smallest known seed in ancient times, and was considered a weed. Ancient Palestine is a dusty and rocky place and before planting could occur, the rocks needed to be removed from the soil.*

Concepts: *Seeds, Fertility, God's Word, Good News, Reaping & Sowing, Nurture, Potential*

Children's Corner:

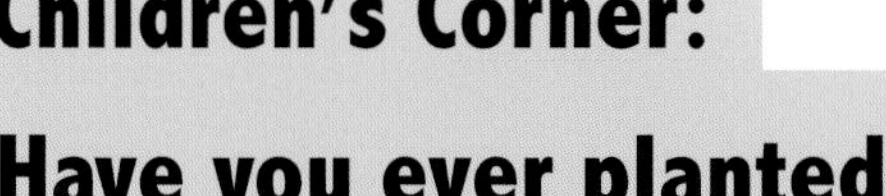

Have you ever planted something and watched it grow? You are growing too. How fast does a person grow?

What do you do each day to make sure you grow up physically healthy and strong? What are some of the things you do to grow your mind? What can you do to grow your heart and spirit?

HUNGER *(The Feeding Stories)*

Mark 6:32-44; Matthew 14:13-21; Luke 9:10-17; John 6:5-13; Mark 8:1-10; Matthew 15:32-38; Matthew 25:34-40

Points to Ponder:

For what do you hunger? What is missing in your life?

How would you define having "just enough?" Does God always provides what we need?

How does that conflict with what we want? Do we live in a world of scarcity or abundance?

What is consumerism? How does consumerism drive our society? Does our society share its blessings? Do our groups and organizations practice exclusion or inclusion? How do you feed other's hunger by meeting the needs of the marginalized?

Becoming a disciple is a process that takes a lifetime of practice. When we change our hearts, we change the world. How is that?

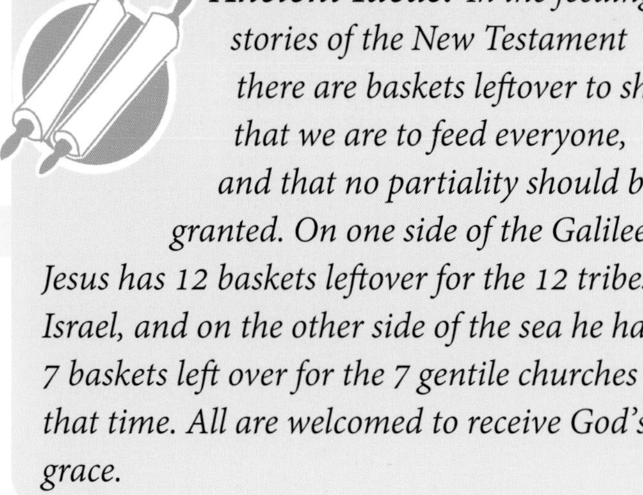

Ancient Ideas: *In the feeding stories of the New Testament there are baskets leftover to show that we are to feed everyone, and that no partiality should be granted. On one side of the Galilee Jesus has 12 baskets leftover for the 12 tribes of Israel, and on the other side of the sea he has 7 baskets left over for the 7 gentile churches at that time. All are welcomed to receive God's grace.*

Concepts: *Hunger, Feeding, Inclusion, Enough, Contentment, Scarcity, Abundance, Empathy, Servant, Stewardship, Service, Love*

Children's Corner:

Many people in the world go to bed hungry each night. Why do you think that happens?

If we have 12 children and 12 apples but one child takes six apples, what happens? Do you want to be the child with 6 apples or none? Can we have not enough or too much? What do you think you have? Do you know what the difference is between wanting something and needing something? What can we do to share our gifts and blessings with others?

LOST AND FOUND (*Luke's Parables of the Lost*)
Luke 15:1-32; Luke 19:9-10

Points to Ponder:

What does it feel like to be lost? And found? Do you ever feel disoriented in the world at times? What happens when we feel fear or depression?

What is God's response to God's lost children? In the Parable of the Prodigal Son, which son are you?

If you knew you could never really be lost, what would that mean for the way you would live your life?

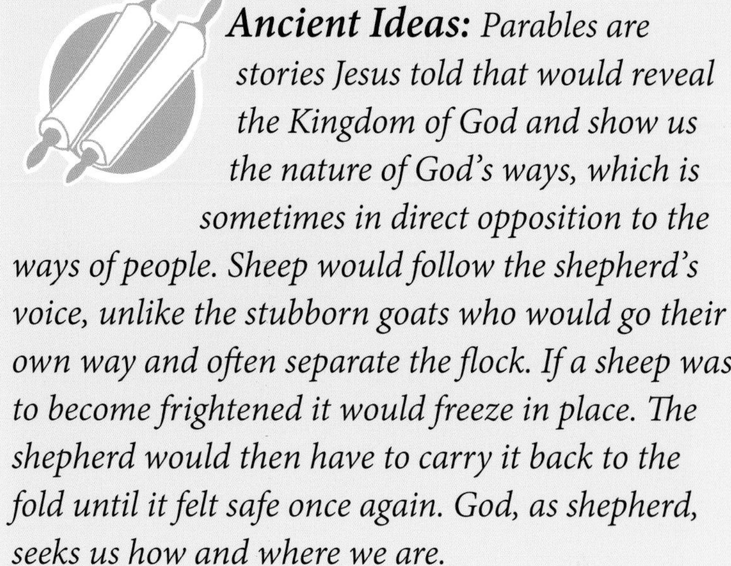

Ancient Ideas: *Parables are stories Jesus told that would reveal the Kingdom of God and show us the nature of God's ways, which is sometimes in direct opposition to the ways of people. Sheep would follow the shepherd's voice, unlike the stubborn goats who would go their own way and often separate the flock. If a sheep was to become frightened it would freeze in place. The shepherd would then have to carry it back to the fold until it felt safe once again. God, as shepherd, seeks us how and where we are.*

Concepts: *Lost, Alone, Afraid, Found, Worthy, Accepted, Unconditional Love, Joy, Hope*

Children's Corner:

Have you ever been lost? Alone? Afraid? How did that make you feel?

Does it help knowing that your parents will always seek to find you wherever you may be? Does it help to know that they love you no matter what?

FORGIVEN (The Story of the Adulterer)

Hosea 6:6; Matthew 7:1-5; Matthew 9:2-13; John 8:3-11;

Points to Ponder:

Shame is a powerful feeling. Do you have things you are ashamed of? Have you ever done something wrong? How did you feel?

What are the seven deadly sins? Why are they deadly? The seven deadly sins are born of our ego. How are Ego and evil linked? Why does sin separate us from God and one another?

What does it feel like to be forgiven? What does it feel like to forgive someone else? What does it feel like to forgive yourself?

What is the difference between conditional and unconditional love?

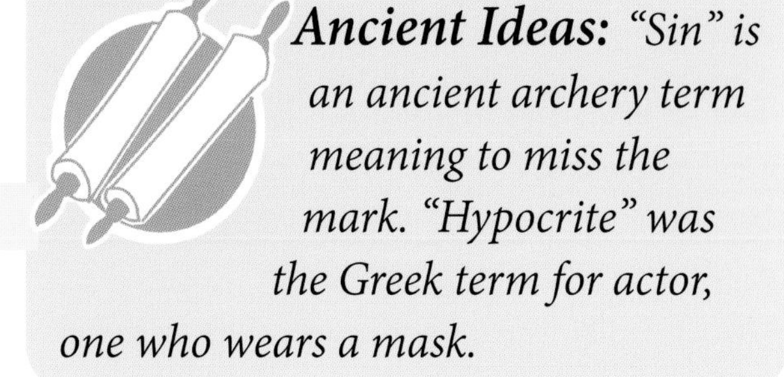

Ancient Ideas: *"Sin" is an ancient archery term meaning to miss the mark. "Hypocrite" was the Greek term for actor, one who wears a mask.*

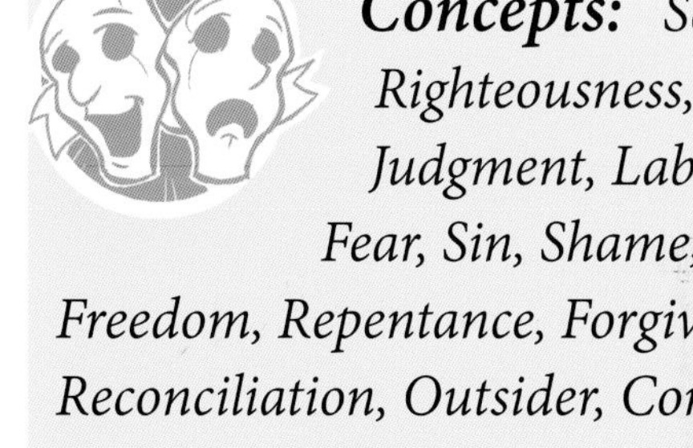

Concepts: *Self-Righteousness, Judgment, Labels, Fear, Sin, Shame, Freedom, Repentance, Forgiveness, Reconciliation, Outsider, Compassion, Love, Acceptance, Grace*

Children's Corner:

Have you ever done anything so wrong that you felt ashamed or embarrassed to tell anyone? What happened when you were caught? How does it feel to be truthful and then to be forgiven?

Have you ever felt like you didn't belong? Does doing something wrong separate you from your family and from your community?

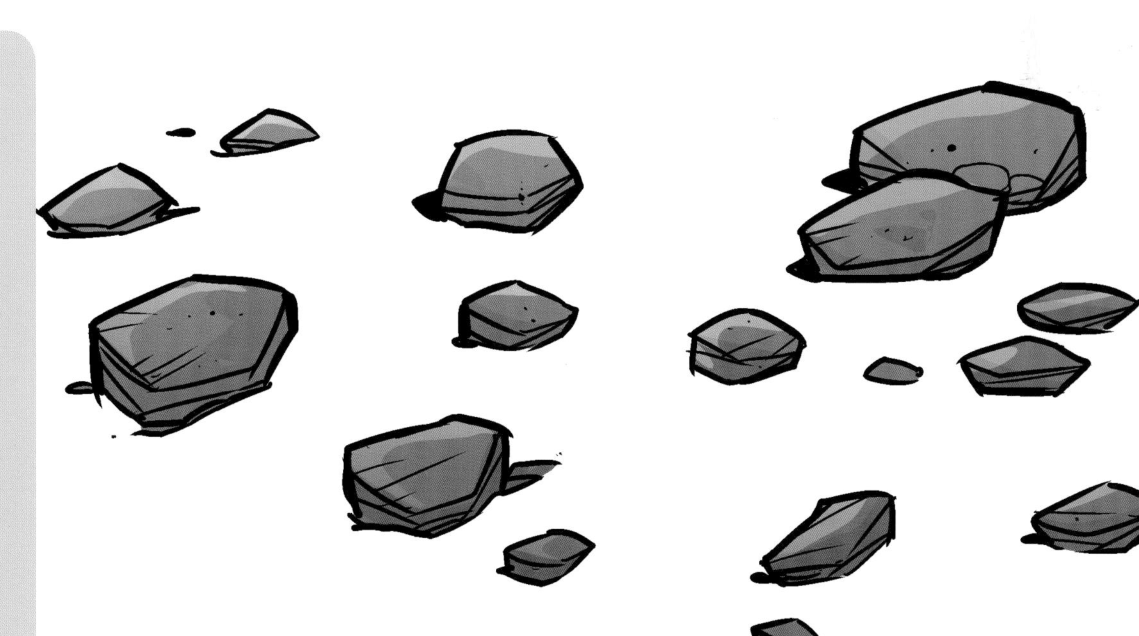

WHO ARE YOU – WHO AM I (*Jesus' Discourse to His Disciples at Caesarea Philippi*)

Matthew 16:13-27; Mark 8:27-38

Points to Ponder:

What does it cost to follow Jesus? How do the ways of people conflict with the ways of God? How are they the same? How do you describe God, the Spirit, and Jesus for yourself? How are you in sync or out of sync with the ways of the world and the ways of the Kingdom of God? Who is God in your life?

What is idolatry? Can God be an idol? What do you worship in your life? What do you spend most of your time focused on? How do you balance competing demands and how do you manage your physical, mental, and spiritual well-being?

What does the word Church mean to you?

Children's Corner:

Are your things more important to you than people?

What do you like to do with your time? What are you good at?

Who or what do you think God is? What do you think the word "church" means? When do you "do" church? How do you "do" church?

Ancient Ideas: *The concept of the underworld and hell were based on real places in the ancient world.* ***Gehenna*** *was actually the burning trash dump outside the walls of Jerusalem, and* ***Hades*** *(Greek) was where Jesus looked out upon the gates of* ***Hades*** *in Caesarea Philippi (Caesarea Philippi was the Roman city north of the little towns where the disciples lived). The river Jordan was fed by the waters that began at the temple. It was a shrine to the Greek and Roman fertility god Pan. It was here that Jesus took his disciples for their graduation. He showed them how he expected them to "do" church.* ***Eklessia*** *(Greek) means church and calls others to action; it is a verb, not a noun!*

Concepts: *Discipleship, Church, Idols, Truth, Perception, Action*

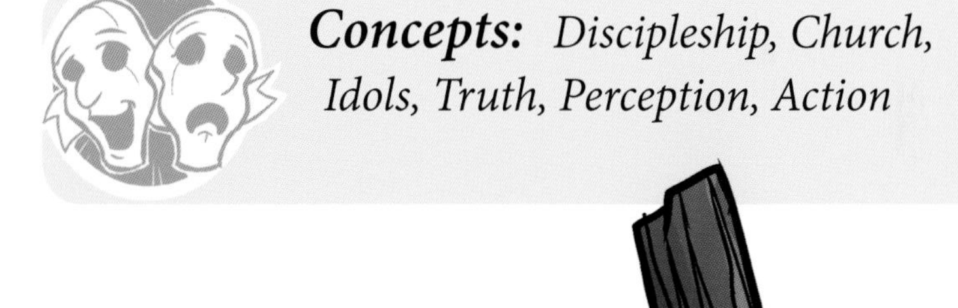

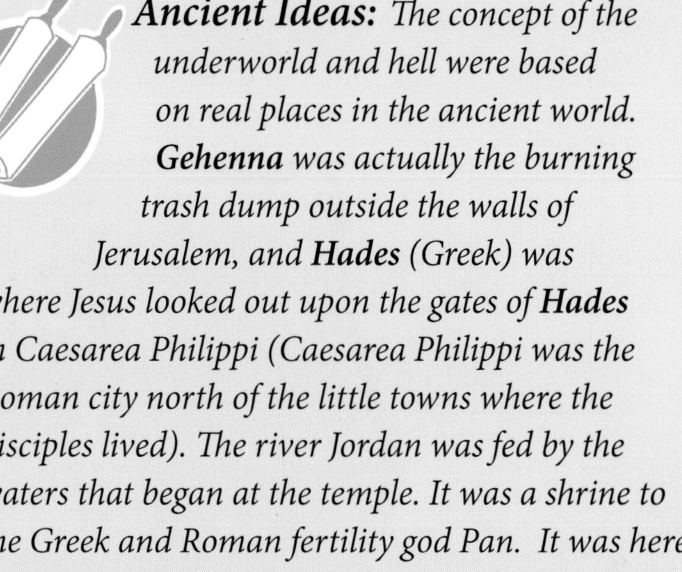

ALL IN *(The Widow's Mite)*

Luke 21:1-4; Mark 12:41-44; Mark 10:17-27; Matthew 6:19-21

Points to Ponder:

Why does Jesus spend so much time talking about stuff? How much time do you spend on your stuff?

Sometimes to affect meaningful change in our lives we just need to start behaving "as if" we were already changed. What do you spend most of your time doing? Where is your heart? How does the widow model a generous heart?

What does it mean to be "all in" for God? Are you truly present with your family, friends, neighbors, and any activities you are doing? Are you able to "unplug" and relate to God and others through worldly possessions?

Ancient Ideas: *The Aramaic word* ***Mammon*** *meant wealth and all that you possessed. Jesus talks a lot about material possessions and notes that they are not good or bad in themselves. It depends what place your stuff holds in your heart relative to God and to one another.*

Concepts: *Status, Wealth, Power, Idols, Ego, Humble, Authentic, Generosity, Treasures, Commitment*

Children's Corner:

What do we mean when we tell you to pay attention? You are at your best when you are paying attention. Is there a time when you put all your effort into something? What happened? How did you feel?

Were you ever present for a pet or a person who really needed your help? How did they feel?

How important is your stuff? Can you live without your favorite things?

THE FIRST SUPPER *(The Last Supper)*

Luke 22:7-27; Matthew 26:26-30; John 13:1-17; John 6:48-51; John 15:5-17

Points to Ponder:

All cultures value mealtime. Why? What can you do to make meals a sacred event to connect you to God, your family, and to others? The cosmic and sublime are acted out every time we share a meal together. What might that mean?

How is the Eucharist enacted in the Christian faith? Why is it so important? In order for us all to live, something first must die. Discuss.

Will a servant or king bring about the Kingdom of God? Why does sacrifice and love rather than power and might usher in God's kingdom?

How does thinking "I get to" rather than "I have to" change your perspective?

Ancient Ideas:

Diakaneos *is a Greek word meaning to serve, and translates into the modern word "deacon". Bread is still sacred in the Middle East and symbolizes life. Bethlehem actually translates as the House of Bread.*

Concepts: *Service, Sacrifice, Community, Meal, Life from Death, Appreciation, Blessing, Eucharist - Communion*

Children's Corner:

What do you eat? Was your food alive once? Does the death of something you ate cause health and life in you? Do you eat regularly with your family? Why is that important?

Why do we sometimes pray before eating? What does gratitude and appreciation mean?

It Is Done (Jesus' Death Upon the Cross)

Matthew 27:45-54; Mark 15:33-39; Luke 23:44-49; John 19:28-30; Luke 14:27

Points to Ponder:

Have you ever paid someone else's debt? What does it mean to sacrifice something?

What does Jesus mean when he says to take up your cross and follow Him?

Have you ever felt betrayed and forsaken? Can fear cause you to feel alone? Does God seem distant or absent from your life sometimes?

How do you view death? How are death and life related?

Ancient Ideas: *The cross was a Roman instrument of torture and humiliation. The Hebrew* ***shofar****, traditionally a ram's horn, would have been blow at 3PM that day, the moment when the Passover lamb was killed for the whole nation. The Lamb of God dies at the instant of the Temple sacrifice.*

Concepts*: Unconditional Love, Unconditional Forgiveness, Sacrifice, Suffering, Death, Forsaken, Absence, Abandoned, Innocence*

Children's Corner:

Have you ever lost something precious to you? Has a pet or anyone close to you ever died? How does that make you feel?

What does it mean to sacrifice something for someone else?

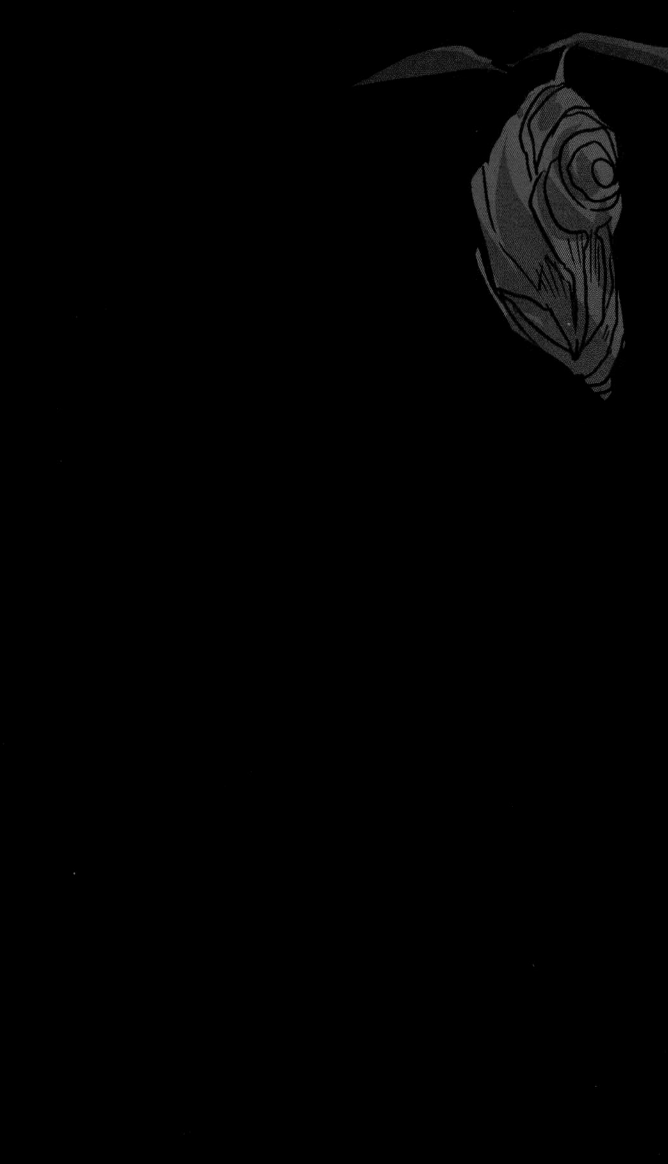

NO WHERE

(Luke 14:27)

NOW HERE

(John 12:23-26)

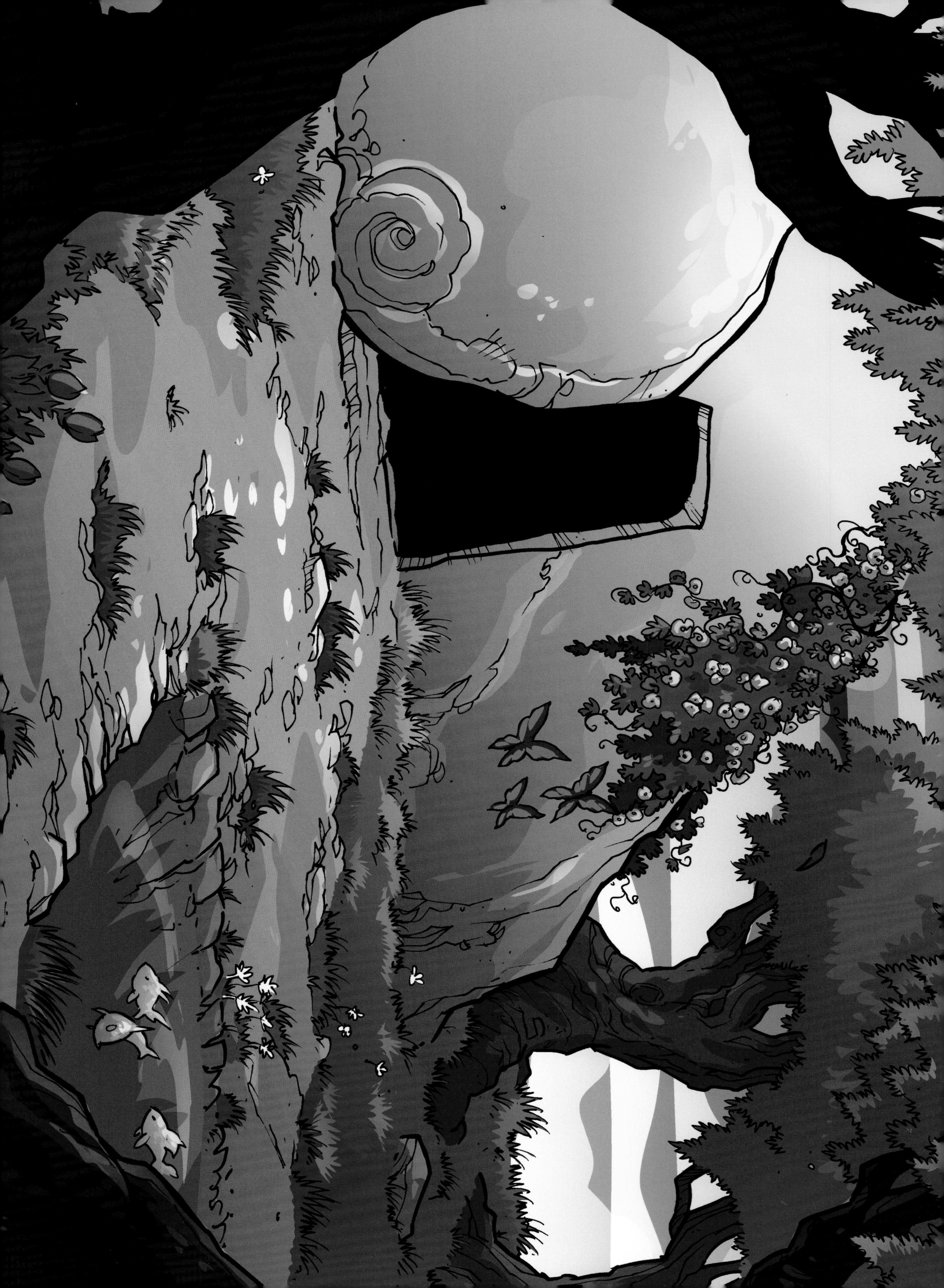

It Is Begun (*The Resurrection*)

John 12:23-26; Matthew 28:1-10; Mark 16:1-8; Luke 24:1-9; John 20:1-20

Points to Ponder:

How does nature hint at the resurrection? What does it mean to be a new creation?

Why don't you think the disciples recognized Jesus?

What does "everlasting life" mean to you?

Does Jesus' sacrifice keep us from experiencing death? What do you think death is?

What is heaven and where is it?

Children's Corner:

What comes after the season of winter? What happens in the springtime? Does a seed look like a tree or does a caterpillar look like a butterfly? How does this relate to Jesus overcoming death? What is a new creation?

What and where is Heaven?

Ancient Ideas: *Hallelujah means to joyfully praise* **YHWH**, *God the Creator.* ***Zoe Aionios,*** *translated as eternal life, really means the Life of the Age to Come, the Life of the Coming Kingdom, or generically, Life to Come.*

Concepts: *Redemption, Resurrection, Transformation, Re-Creation, Re-Connection, New Life*

Wind and Fire *(Pentecost)*
John 20:21-22; Acts 2:1-4; 1 Corinthians 12:4-27

Points to Ponder:

What or who do you think the Holy Spirit is?

We all have different gifts and talents. Is one better than another? What are your gifts and talents?

You are the temple where God now dwells. Do you believe that? Why? What is your idea of Church as the Body of Christ? Is our society serving or self-serving?

Ancient Ideas: *"Apostle" means messenger or envoy – one who is sent. For Jesus, His students were sent to serve, to find the lost, feed the hungry, and to spread the Gospel message of Christ - the good news of God's love for all his children!*

Concepts: *Holy Spirit, Gifts, Discipleship, Service, Body of Christ, Church*

Children's Corner:

What or who do you think the Holy Spirit is?

What do you really like doing? What are you gifts and talents? Are your friends good at different things? Is it better to have everyone good at the same thing or different things? Why? Have you ever been on a team? How were everyone's different talents or skills used?

What do you think God's Church should be? How do we serve one another together?

Blind, But Now I See (*Saul's Conversion*)

Acts 9:1-22; John 9:25; Isaiah 42:5-7

Points to Ponder:

Paul was a passionate man and zealous in his beliefs. Is it possible that self-righteousness can blind us?

Imagine seeing one another as God sees us…is that possible? How would that make us treat one another?

Do we all have prejudices and blind spots? What are yours?

What does it mean to be self-aware? What can you do about opening the eyes of your heart?

Ancient Ideas: *The Bible uses blindness to show that even though someone can physically see, they could still be blind in spirit. Jesus, through His teachings, tries to open the "eyes" of our hearts. Naming someone in the Bible often showed possession. When God changed someone's name, God took ownership of the person. Saul believed he was doing God's will. After he saw things differently, God changed his name to Paul and focused his passion and talents on spreading the Gospel to the rest of the world outside of Jerusalem.*

Concepts: *Blindness, Repent, Self- Righteousness, Judgment, Self-Aware, Passion, Purpose, Focus, Apostle*

Children's Corner:

What is right and wrong? What is good and bad? Have you ever done something wrong or bad? Does that make you a bad person? Once you see what you did wrong, how do you change for next time? Can you grow from making mistakes and changing?

Can we see things from more than one point of view? What does it mean to see things differently?

Behold (*The Burning Bush*)

Exodus 3:1-15; Psalm 8; Isaiah 7:14; Philippians 4:4-9; Revelations 1:8

Points to Ponder:

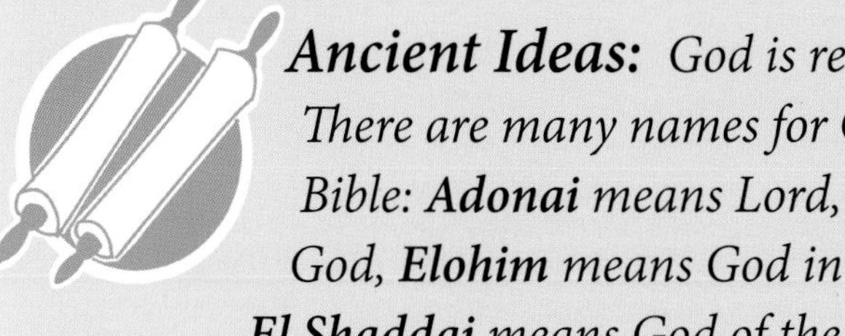

How can one find God? There is no word for faith in Hebrew; it is more like trust. Why is that so? Is it more important to believe in God or experience God?

Discipleship is more of a posture, a way of seeing things, of experiencing things. Are there burning bushes all around us but we are moving too fast to see them? Is the ground upon which you are standing Holy ground? There is also no word for spiritual in Hebrew because that would mean some things are spiritual while others are not. Is it possible that everything is spiritual?

Can you see the extraordinary in the ordinary?

Once you experience the indiscriminate mercy, grace, and love of God, how then do we extend this to others?

Children's Corner:

Where is God? Is God up or down, inside or outside? How is God with us?

Which side of the telescope do you look through? What happens when we turn it around? Which way should you hold the telescope to see God? We cannot comprehend the mind of God, but we can experience the heart of God. Discuss!

Ancient Ideas: *God is relational. There are many names for God in the Bible:* ***Adonai*** *means Lord,* ***El*** *means God,* ***Elohim*** *means God in the plural,* ***El Shaddai*** *means God of the mountain,* ***Abba*** *means Daddy,* ***Immanuel*** *means God with us.* ***YHWH*** *is the unutterable name - it may resemble the act of breathing.* ***Ehyeh Asher Ehyeh*** *is translated as a verb meaning I will be that, what, who, which, where I will be. It is this name that God spoke to Moses, as an active manifestation of divine existence revealing that God cannot be contained by time or place.*

Concepts: *Belief, Trust, Open, Seeing the Sacred, I Am Everything/ Everywhere, God with Us*

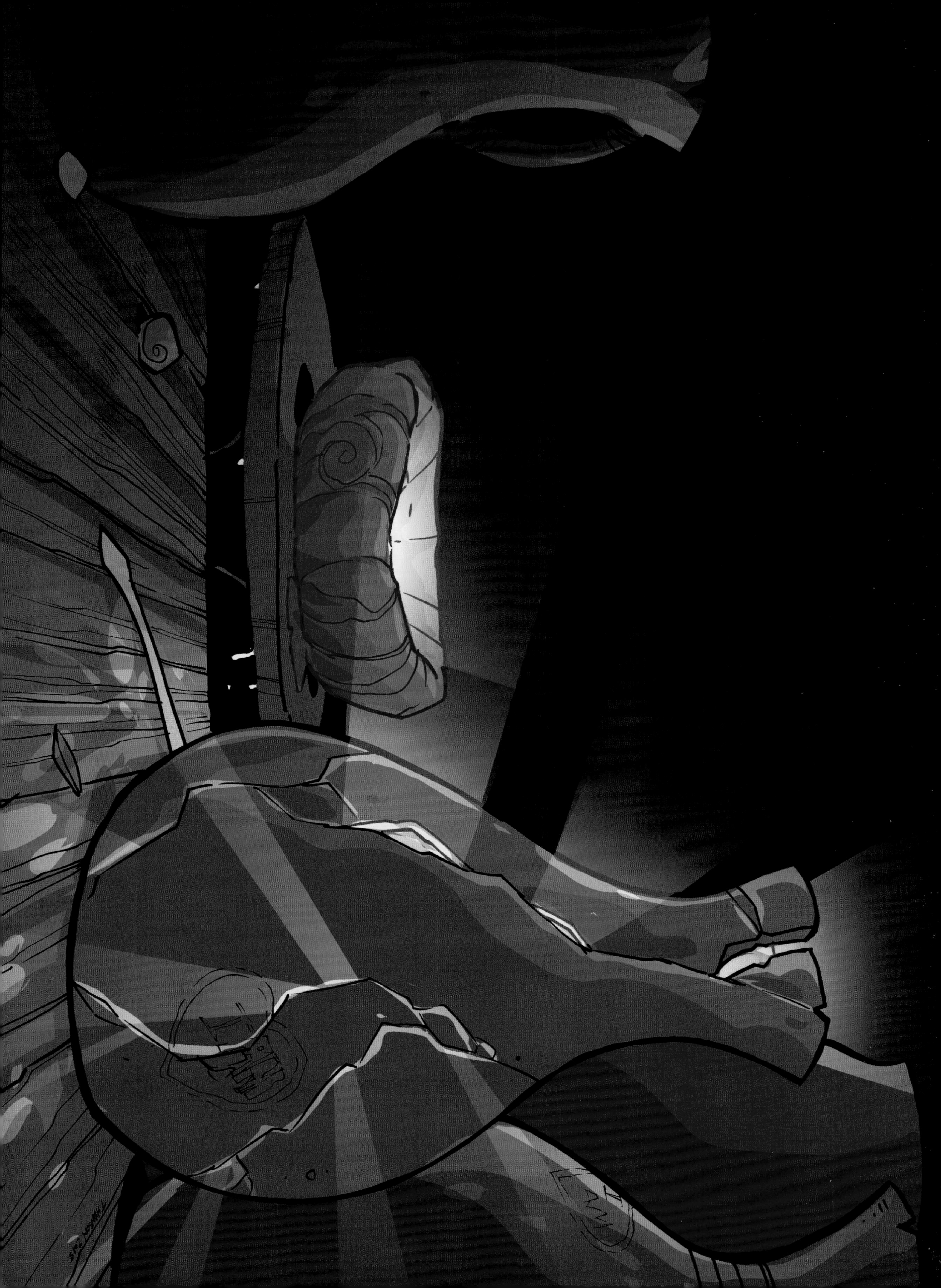

Fragile Vessels (*Jars of Clay*)

Isaiah 64:8; 2 Corinthians 4:6-7; 1 Corinthians 13:1-13

Points to Ponder:

How do we shine Jesus' light in the world? How do we hide that light? Only light can drive out darkness and only love can drive out fear. Why is love the most important thing there is? Why is sharing that love as important?

Why is much of how we view the world and others an illusion? Can the ego trick us into thinking the vessel is more important than the contents? How does our society contribute to that viewpoint?

Ancient Ideas: **Kenosis** *is a Greek word meaning to empty one's self to make room for God. We cease to impose our will and are now open to God's will in our lives.*

Concepts*: Broken, Inner Light, Life, Love, Spirit, Body of Christ, Selfish/Selfless, Labels & Prejudice, Busyness, Ego*

Children's Corner:

What is the purpose of a container? What happens if the container is broken?

Do people come in different shapes and sizes? What makes someone special: what's on the inside or the outside? Is anyone perfect?

Why is love so important? Once you are filled with God's love, what can you do with that?

GO WITH ME (*Discipleship*)

Mark 10:13-16; Matthew 19:13-15; Matthew 18:1-5; Luke 18:15-17; John 8:31; John 14:12-14; John 21:15-19

Points to Ponder:

Why does Jesus say to gain the kingdom of heaven, you must be like a child? What is the difference between being childlike and childish? Jesus knew people's hearts and He cared more for where a person's heart was than the person's status. Why? It's not about the head; it's about the heart. Do you believe that if you change your heart, you change the world? In what way? Can you control the world or just your view of it?

What does it mean to be a disciple of Christ? ***Ubuntu*** is an African greeting that translates as "the god in me recognizes the god in you." Can you see God in others? Do others see God in you? How do we carry and bring the love of Jesus to broken people and a broken world? We may not have all the answers, but we have to keep asking the questions; and hopefully along the way we do it with love.

"Preach the gospel at all times, and when necessary use words." - St. Francis of Assisi

Children's Corner:

What does the word humble mean?

You spend a lot of time in school. Why is that important? Do we ever finish learning?

Who do people follow today? Who or what do you follow? What does following Jesus mean? How is that different? Do your life and actions reflect your words?

Ancient Ideas: *A disciple (a* ***Talmid****) had to be a lifelong student with a childlike wonder open to learning and seeing the world anew. It is about the journey and living with passion. The disciple also realizes that learning never ends and therefore tries to maintain a humble and open posture at all times. Discipleship is a process and is lived through culture and through community, not apart from it.*

Concepts: *Childlike, Discipleship, Humble, Student, Wonder, Love, Connections, Point of View, Evangelize, Conversion, Open, Transformation*

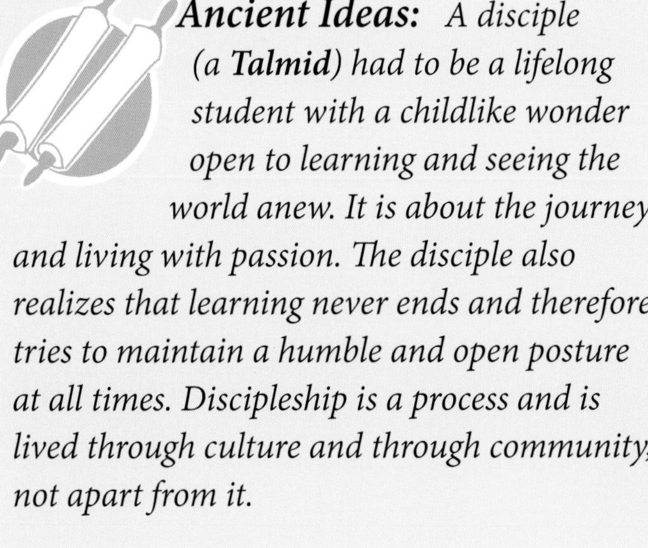

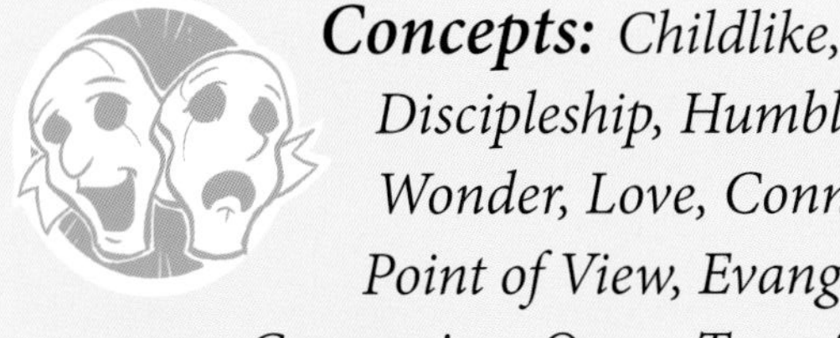

The Beginning...

Love God (Deuteronomy 6:5)
Love One Another (John 13:34-35)
Go and Make Disciples of ALL and Know That I Am With You Always (Matthew 28:19-20)

(1 John 3:1-2)

"You Are the Light of the World." (Mathew 5:14-16)

Notes on Colors and Symbols:

Colors:

White – *Eternal Life, Purity*

Black – *The Absence of Life*

Blue – *The Kingdom of God, Inner Spirit and Divinity, God's Touch*

Purple – *Royalty, Kingship, Power*

Green – *The Natural World, Fertility and Life*

Red – *Humanity and The Ways of Man*

Yellow – *Sadness, Misfortune*

Orange (red & yellow) – *The Human Condition*

Symbols:

The Natural Light *in each picture represents God the Creator (will generally begin at the left)*

God the Spirit *is represented by a White Dove or Wind*

The Serpent (and the Diamond Pattern) – *Human Nature, The Ego, Evil*

Black Sheep – *The Lost Children of God*

The Children – *Disciples of Jesus (then and now)*

The Fish – *Christianity*

Butterflies – *New Creation, Transformation, Resurrection*

Swirl - *The Fingerprints of God Found in All of Creation*

The Rainbow – *God's Promise, Covenant*

Clothing – *Note the Colors Worn*

The Heart Symbol *with the words I AM inside it – symbolizes God coming to us and also our response to God." I Am Here" is how God is present with us, and "Here I Am" is how we reciprocate by opening our hearts to God; creating a space and a place for the Spirit of God to dwell within us. This surrender and partnership is at the Heart of Discipleship.*

About the Author:

The Rev. Carmen J. Viola is a deacon in the Episcopal Church of the Diocese of New Jersey. He lives in New Jersey with his wife and youngest child where he loves serving God and showing others how to have a deeper relationship with God and one another. Visit Carmen at www.heartofdiscipleship.com

About the Illustrator:

Travis Hanson is an Eisner nominated fantasy illustrator with a huge imagination. His works include comics, children's art, fantasy and just fun illustrations that encourages the need for people to be creative. Visit Travis Hanson at www.beanleafpress.com

There are no coincidences; only God-incidences! Two years ago I purchased an illustrated book on living your dreams, by Travis Hanson. I really connected with the artist's vision and drawings, so much so that, two weeks later, I found myself literally dreaming Travis' art style into several biblical pictures. Not knowing Travis personally, I instead reached out to other artists I did know to try and recreate my vision, but couldn't quite find the right fit, and the dream stalled.

For the next two years, I occupied myself with work, family, and church, leaving little time for dreams. During this time, I came home every day feeling drained by my hectic schedule, so I reincorporated exercise into my life, hoping it would give me the boost I needed. I had ridden my bike often in the past, so I searched online for bike trails —lo and behold, there was a bike trail through the woods just around the corner from my home. I had lived there for seven years without ever once noticing the trail! I started riding my bike again, and my energy quickly returned, allowing me to devote more time to my physical, mental, and spiritual self– I felt great for the first time in years.

During this "rejuvenation process," I was browsing Facebook one day when I saw a post by Travis Hanson, the artist of the illustration book that had inspired my dreams two years ago. He indicated that he was searching for creative projects, so I emailed him, and he called me back. A few minutes into our conversation, I knew that Travis was the artist for my vision. There was an instant energy and connection between us. He too was a lifelong active Christian. I got an immediate sense that everything would come together. I told Travis that I only had a few pictures developed, but he suggested that we needed more along the lines of 30 images if we were going to create a whole book!

What happened next was uncanny. The following three weeks I woke up almost every night, writing my dreams in a notebook by my bedside. Then on my bike rides I continued to daydream and cultivate these visions. Within a month, I had created enough pictures and concepts for a whole book on discipleship. At the same time, I received a call from someone telling me she had been praying for me, that the Holy Spirit would guide me, and that I would have the strength to do God's will. The timing couldn't have been more amazing – she knew nothing about the journey I was on – it was clear now that God was calling for me (literally!) to finish this book. I called Travis to tell him what had transpired, and that we needed to accelerate development. I still wasn't sure how to finance it, but with God all things are possible.

Thankfully, my wife, bless her, unconditionally supported this daunting undertaking. And God continued sending much needed help. A webmaster friend of mine offered to develop the website. Then I met with a fellow deacon and his wife for lunch and during our conversation, brought up the book and all of the coincidences that surrounded this effort. His wife looked me in the eyes and asked if I knew what they did for a living –she told me that they market Christian books.

We have a saying at our church: "God is good, all the time!" My journey as I've described it above is certainly proof of that! Travis's tagline at his website is, "This is your story, your dream, your adventure. Let's bring it to life!" To be honest, this book was more like an inspired vision than a dream and this story really isn't mine, it's ours...and the rest as they say is "His Story!"

Your Faithful Servent,
The Rev. Carmen J. Viola, Deacon